# The Ultimate Guidebook for Cat Owners

(from a veterinarian)

# The Ultimate Guidebook for Cat Owners

## (from a veterinarian)

How to choose, care for, and keep happy, healthy kittens and cats

**Dr. Marlena Lopez** BSc DVM

Smith Street Books

# Introduction

Welcoming a cat into your life is a journey of companionship, love, and a touch of mystery. Cats fascinate us with their special personalities, habits, and quirks. Whether you're a seasoned cat owner or considering adopting your first feline friend, this book is here to provide you with the knowledge and tools you need to create a happy and healthy life for your cat.

*The Ultimate Guidebook for Cat Owners* is designed to cover every stage of a cat's life, from playful kittens to dignified seniors. You'll find advice on selecting the right cat for your family, understanding cat behavior, and navigating essential aspects of feline health and care, such as vaccinations, dental hygiene, and weight management. There's also guidance on how to create a stress-free environment for your cat, interpret their body language, and address common concerns like inappropriate urination or feline arthritis.

As a veterinarian with a background in general practice and shelter medicine, I've dedicated my career to improving animal welfare and helping pet owners strengthen their bonds with their pets. My work in veterinary clinics has fueled my passion for educating pet owners, and I have seen firsthand how the right information can transform the lives of cats and their families. This book is an extension of my mission to empower pet owners with the knowledge they need to build a lasting, rewarding bond with their cats.

With *The Ultimate Guidebook for Cat Owners*, you'll be well equipped to ensure a lifetime of love, happiness, and health for your feline friend.

# 1

# Getting a Cat: What Age is Right for You?

You've decided to get a cat: congrats! You're embarking on a journey of love and companionship. But which cat should you get? By evaluating your lifestyle and home, you can decide if a kitten or an adult will suit your family.

Many people like the idea of watching their pet grow up. Kittens can be a lot of fun, but they also require more time, attention, and veterinary care, especially over the first six months. Kittens require constant supervision, and you may need to kitten proof your home from common dangers such as electrical wires. If you have the time and energy to devote, a kitten may be a good option for you.

Adult cats may be a good choice if you want a cat that's out of the kitten stage and a bit calmer. Adult cats may be a good option for a household with children, as they are generally more mature and patient. They may also be the right choice if you are a busy, working family or a senior citizen looking for companionship without a kitten's high energy and maintenance. With an adult cat, you know exactly what you're getting, from looks to personality.

Senior cats are more emotionally mature and independent. They can be more vulnerable to illness, but owners of any aged cat should be vigilant about their health. If you lead a relaxed lifestyle, a senior cat may be the perfect fit.

# 2

# Caring for a Kitten

Cats are considered kittens from birth to six months of age.

Starting at six to eight weeks of age, and ending at 16–20 weeks, they receive a series of three vaccines. These appointments are vital to protect your kitten against infectious diseases, and to provide an opportunity for your veterinarian to examine your kitten and make sure they are in optimum health.

To support their health, it's important to feed a kitten food specially formulated for their age. They are in a period of rapid growth and have increased nutritional requirements for protein, as well as vitamins and minerals, including vitamin D and calcium.

Once they've reached around four months of age, it's widely recommended that cats are spayed or neutered to prevent unwanted pregnancies and behaviors associated with sexual maturity.

Kittens usually learn how to use a litter tray by copying their mother from three to eight weeks of age. You may just need to show your kitten where their litter tray is or encourage them to use it by placing them in the tray after mealtimes or when your kitten shows signs of needing a toilet such as sniffing, scratching, or beginning to crouch.

From an early age, teaching positive associations with being groomed is a good idea; you can start by using a small brush or even a soft-bristled toothbrush to gently stroke your kitten, rewarding calm behavior with praise and a treat.

At any age, kittens are very playful. Engaging them in play activities will keep them occupied and exercised while strengthening your bond.

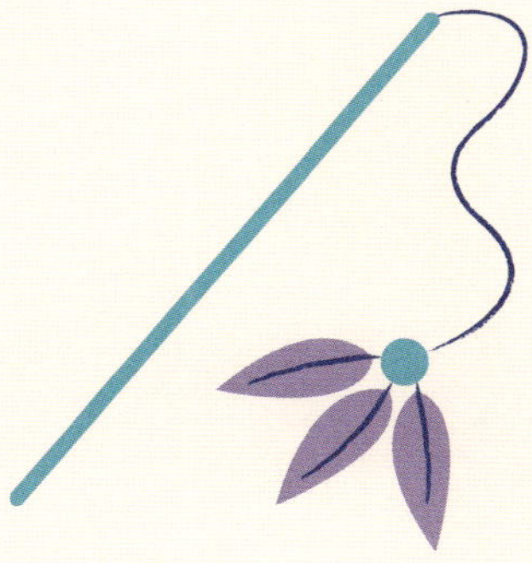

# 3

# Caring for a Junior & Adult Cat

Cats are considered juniors from seven months to two years of age.

Young cats are more active and enjoy exploring, which can lead to problems related to fighting, trauma, and hunting; an indoor-only lifestyle will reduce these risks. During this transitional life stage, they will start growing out of rambunctious kitten behavior and learn how to behave more like an adult cat.

As cats mature into adults and stop growing, their metabolism slows down; regular weight monitoring is important during this stage. Junior cats are also at a great age to implement a dental care routine.

Parasite control, vaccinations, dental health, nutrition, and weight management are important in the adult life stage. Cats are considered adults from three to six years and mature from seven to ten years of age.

Common problems seen in adult cats include obesity, dental disease, bladder disorders, intestinal diseases, and behavioral problems. As cats enter the mature age group, the risk of certain age-related disorders starts to increase, so it's important to regularly visit your veterinarian for health examinations.

# 4

# Caring for a Senior Cat

Cats are considered seniors from the age of 11–14 years and super seniors from 15 years of age. Senior cats need vigilant attention, as well as regular health checks, as they are at increased risk of developing kidney disease, arthritis, an overactive thyroid, high blood pressure, diabetes, and cancer. Consult a veterinarian if you notice these signs in your senior cat: sleeping all the time, confusion, difficulty or reluctance jumping/climbing or using their litter tray, unintentional weight loss or gain, lumps on the body, behavioral changes, and changes in their appetite, thirst, and toileting patterns.

Senior cats may develop skin and coat problems due to reduced grooming. Their nails may become overgrown if they stop using their scratching posts. You can help your senior maintain their personal grooming needs by brushing them at least once a week and trimming their nails every few weeks.

Older cats may become dehydrated and constipated, and diseases such as an overactive thyroid, kidney disease, and diabetes may exacerbate this issue. Feeding your senior cat wet food may help increase their water intake.

Many of the diseases affecting senior cats can be cured or managed. It's important to avoid dismissing changes as just old age. While older cats are more likely to develop certain diseases, many issues are very treatable.

**TIP**

Provide regular vet check-ups, cozy bedding, and joint supplements to keep your senior cat comfortable and thriving.

# 5

# Finding Reliable Sources of Information

When examining information, it's important to evaluate the reliability of the source, including their education, work experience, and credentials. Veterinary professionals not only undergo extensive education to become licensed, but they are also required to undertake continuing education to learn and discover viable ways to improve on patient care. The best care for your pet is provided as a partnership between your vet clinic and your family.

Social media and the internet can provide pet owners with great information. However, anyone can create a platform and share pet health information, whether they have the qualifications or not. Blogs, websites, and social media pages run by laypeople or individuals with no formal nutrition training or education are unreliable resources.

There are some informed and responsible breeders out there, but it's important for pet owners to remember: breeders do not go to medical school and should not offer medical advice. A good breeder will have a working relationship with a veterinarian who will examine the breeder's kittens and give them an initial vaccination prior to the kittens joining their new family.

# 6

# Pet Insurance

Whether for humans or animals, the cost of health care is high. Human health care is heavily subsidized by governments and health insurance, concealing the true cost of medicine from the patients.

Veterinary care is provided by private businesses, which do not receive the same financial support; to take care of pets properly, owners will have to pay veterinary fees that can be difficult to afford.

Pet insurance is designed to protect you and your pet by minimizing the overall cost of veterinary expenses. By agreeing to pay a monthly sum to a pet insurance company, you receive reimbursement for expenses that are covered by the policy.

Insurance will give you peace of mind knowing that you will be financially protected in the event your cat suffers an illness or injury, but it can also help cover the costs of preventative care such as routine check-ups, vaccinations, and dental treatments.

Many pet owners have had to make the difficult decision to euthanize based on financial constraints; insurance will allow you to choose and afford different treatment options and provide life-saving therapies and surgeries.

There is a range of pet insurance providers on the market, and not all policies are created equal. It's important to do your research and compare several different policies to choose one that best aligns with your lifestyle, your cat's breed, and any particular issues that may arise in the future.

**TIP**

Invest in pet insurance early for your cat; it ensures affordable care for unexpected illnesses or injuries later in life.

# 7

# Microchips

Microchipping your cat significantly increases the chance of being reunited if they ever become lost.

A microchip is a radio-frequency transponder and a form of permanent electronic identification. The chip itself is only about the size of a grain of rice. It doesn't require a battery or power and is injected just under the skin between the shoulder blades, in a manner similar to a vaccination. A microchip is not a tracking device; it carries a unique identification number and provides a way for a veterinarian, shelter, or council to contact you if your pet is brought in.

The microchip number is recorded on a database registry with details about the animal and the owner's contact information. It's important for this information to be kept up to date if you move or change phone numbers, so that you will still be contactable should your pet go astray.

Other forms of identification such as tags and collars are also recommended. However, they can break off, be removed, or wear out until they are illegible.

Losing your pet can be terrifying. If your cat were to become lost or stolen, knowing that they have a microchip can provide you with some peace of mind and increase the chance of them returning home to you.

# 8

# Choosing the Right Cat Carrier

A cat carrier will ensure that your cat is safe and comfortable, from the day you bring them home to every journey thereafter, whether it's to the veterinary clinic, on a move, or to the boarding cattery.

Regardless of how long a trip is, your cat or kitten will need to travel in a carrier.

Robust plastic carriers are recommended, as they are less likely to be damaged during transport. Cardboard carriers may get wet or tear, and they are easier for cats to escape from if they become stressed.

Carriers should come apart easily without making loud noises that may startle your cat. Those with a removable top allow your veterinarian to easily examine your cat without having to remove them completely from their safe space. You can pack their carrier with their favorite toys, treats, or blankets to comfort them during travel.

Carriers that allow your cat to walk straight in are great for training your cat to enter voluntarily; this can be done by placing a treat in the carrier.

Integrating the carrier into your home furnishing by placing it in a normal resting spot for your cat, rather than placing it in storage, and rewarding your cat with treats upon entering it will help them associate the carrier with positive experiences. This will make future travel less stressful for everyone and trips to the veterinarian more positive.

# 9

# Keeping Your Cat Happy & Healthy Indoors

Keeping cats indoors is beneficial for their health and wellbeing, as well as the wellbeing of wildlife and owners. Cats living indoors have reduced exposure to multiple health risks and have longer lifespans than free-roaming cats; uncontrolled outdoor access is associated with welfare concerns, including increased risks of disease, parasites, and injury, death due to traffic, predation, or ingestion of toxic substances, and permanent separation from owners.

Free-roaming cats are at an increased risk of contracting infectious diseases from other cats, including feline immunodeficiency virus (FIV) and feline leukemia (FeLV). Cats are also at risk of intestinal worms, consumed as eggs via contaminated soil or infected animals. While all cats should receive regular parasite control, indoor cats have a reduced risk of picking up parasites.

The reduced risk from traffic, falls from buildings, and other outdoor accidents means that keeping your cat indoors will likely reduce vet fees. And sometimes, injuries aren't an accident; some people view outdoor cats as pests and may harm them. Keeping your cat indoors protects them, along with the wildlife populations they pose a serious threat to.

Healthy alternatives to roaming include cat enclosures, enclosed patios, and harness walks. Cats with plenty of horizontal and vertical climbing space, scratching posts, and toys, will have the appropriate outlets to perform their natural behaviors in an environment that is mentally and physically stimulating.

10

# Litter Trays

Litter tray maintenance is an important part of responsible cat ownership. The type of litter tray, its location, how often and what it's cleaned with, and the litter itself are all important factors that influence your cat's toileting habits.

Cats need an adequately sized tray so that they can move around; it should be one and a half times the length of your cat from nose to base of tail. Make sure the litter is deep enough for them to dig in: ideally 3–4 cm (1–1½ inch).

It's recommended to initially use the same type of litter your cat used as a kitten, and then try different kinds until you find their preference by providing different litters at the same time in two trays.

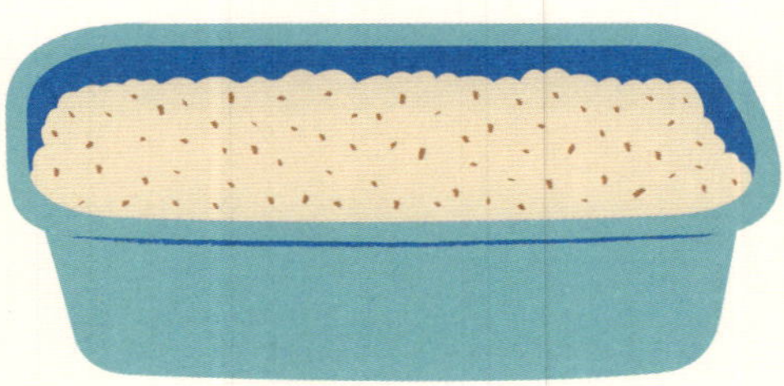

Covered or hooded litter trays leave less mess, but some cats refuse to use them.

The general rule of thumb for the number of required litter trays: one tray per cat plus a spare, as well as a minimum of one tray per story in the home. These should be kept away from eating and sleeping areas, in quiet sections of the house as cats prefer privacy. They like to be able to see people or other animals approaching and have multiple exit routes to escape in a hurry.

Any waste should be scooped out every day. Once a week, their trays should be emptied, washed with unscented soapy warm water, rinsed, and refilled.

If your cat is regularly toileting outside their tray, consult your veterinarian as this may indicate a health problem.

# 11

# Multi-Cat Households

Domestic cats have the capacity to live alone or in groups. Within groups, individual cats will form attachments to certain individuals and actively avoid others.

Long-term stress associated with household conflict can cause your cats serious problems. Outright fighting resulting in injuries such as cat bite abscesses are less common inside the home. But just because cats aren't actively fighting doesn't mean they're not impacted by living together.

Silent conflict may seem subtle, but it can cause significant medical problems. Long-term stress and high levels of cortisol can compromise the immune system, resulting in a recurrence of cat flu and other diseases. It can also cause recurrent inflammation of the bladder and problems with the coat and overgrooming.

Signs of conflict between cats include fighting, chasing, hissing, fleeing from the other cats, growling, spitting, screaming, staring, stalking, crouching, twitching tails, blocking each other, trembling, remaining hidden, or avoidance.

If cats do not want to interact with other cats, it's essential that they can access necessities in a solitary fashion. Food and water bowls, litter trays, marking and scratching posts, and resting areas should be spread throughout the house to increase household harmony.

Synthesized pheromones imitate naturally produced cat pheromones and can be used to promote a sense of calm and security in stressful situations, including conflict between cats in the same household.

A veterinary behaviorist can help identify where conflicts are arising and provide cat owners with the education and tools to help cats cohabitate.

**TIP**

Provide enough resources like litter boxes, food, and hiding spots to reduce tension and promote harmony in multi-cat households.

12

# Reading Cat Body Language

Cats communicate with us and one another using non-verbal language. Understanding cat body language will enable you to interpret what they are feeling. There is no such thing as an aggressive cat, just an animal exhibiting signs of aggression, often stemming from fear.

A cat's body language can be subtle. Examining a cat's eyes, ears, mouth, body posture, and tail can help you understand how they are feeling to keep your cat and everyone else feeling safe and comfortable.

A happy and relaxed cat will stand with a relaxed body posture and tail. If they are lying down, they may lie on their side and expose their belly, which is a sign of trust. Their ears will be in a neutral position, their eyes will have their regular shape, and their mouth will be closed. They may meow or purr.

A fearful cat's body may be tightly crouched with limbs tucked, or they may stand with an arched back, front paw lifted to swipe if needed, the fur on their back and tail raised. Their ears may be flattened, head lowered, pupils dilated, mouth open and tense, tail curled around their body to protect it or held up and rigid. They may show their teeth, growl, or hiss.

# 13

# Dental Care

Dental health is as vital to a cat's wellbeing as it is to human health. Dental disease is one of the most common problems diagnosed in pets: most cats over the age of three years exhibit some level of dental disease.

This can be prevented by establishing a good home care program. The ideal regimen includes daily toothbrushing; other treatments that may be implemented include the use of clinically proven dental diets, gels, rinses, treats, and wipes.

Dental disease can cause bad breath, infection, and pain. It can also lead to serious illness. If left untreated, a serious gum infection can damage the soft tissue, destroy the bone that supports the teeth, and allow bacteria to enter your pet's bloodstream, making them seriously ill. Once in the bloodstream, the bacteria can lodge in small blood vessels (most commonly in the liver or kidneys) and cause life-threatening disease. However, in partnership with your veterinarian, good feline dental health is achievable.

Home care is imperfect, and periodically tartar must be properly removed and the teeth's surface properly polished and disinfected by a veterinarian; this professional cleaning is like dental treatment for humans.

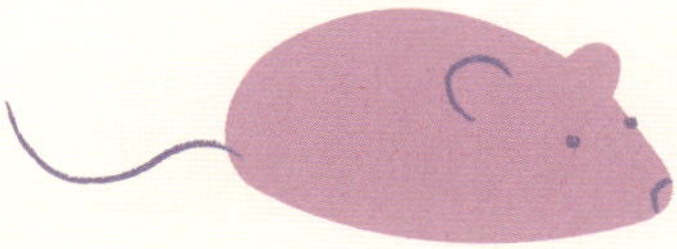

**Dental chews:** The goal of a dental chew is to clean your cat's teeth while providing environmental enrichment. Dental chew treats and toys work by mechanically removing plaque, and some are chemically formulated to create a protective barrier on the teeth's surface.

There are a variety of dental chews that make claims of improving dental health. The Veterinary Oral Health Council is an independent body of veterinary dentists that critically analyze these claims and put their seal of approval on products designed to reduce plaque and tartar. Even approved dental treats should be limited per day, however, as these treats quickly add up in calories.

Other great tools to help remove plaque and tartar include dental wipes, which are easy to gently rub around your cat's teeth and gums, dental rinses, and water additives. These last two coat the entire mouth, including the gums, tongue, and teeth, which freshens the breath and removes plaque.

# 14

# Teething

Just like human babies, kittens are born without teeth. Their baby teeth grow in around two to four weeks of age, and between three and four months these fall out to make room for their permanent adult teeth. Typically, all adult teeth are in place by six to seven months of age.

Your kitten may experience some discomfort during teething – the best way to help is to provide them with soft chew toys that won't damage their teeth.

Signs your kitten is teething include red and inflamed gums. A mild amount of bleeding may occur. You may find their kitten teeth on the floor, although kittens will more commonly swallow them, which is normal and safe.

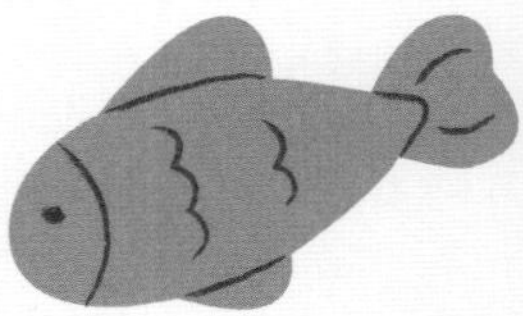

Don’t reward unwanted behavior; if your kitten starts chewing on your hands or household items, offer them a toy instead. At each kitten exam and at the time of spaying or castrating, your vet will assess your kitten’s teeth and look for problems such as crooked teeth, jaw misalignment, fractured teeth, and retained baby teeth leading to overcrowding.

When your kitten is teething, it is a good time to get them used to having their mouth touched and examined.

Make it a positive experience by offering treats each time you touch your kitten’s mouth. This will allow you to introduce a dental care routine early that they will enjoy or at least tolerate.

# 15

# How to Brush Your Cat's Teeth

To introduce a dental routine, choose a time and place where your cat is calm. For the first few sessions, start by placing a small amount of cat toothpaste on your finger and offering it for your cat to lick, or place a small amount on their nose to introduce them to the flavor. Don't use human toothpastes: they contain ingredients that may be toxic to cats. Cat toothpaste comes in flavors that are designed to be tasty and appealing to cats.

Progress to lifting your cat's lips until they are comfortable – from this point on, it's easiest to position them with their back facing you for better control. For the next few days, apply some toothpaste to a cotton bud and gently rub it on their teeth in a circular motion.

It's important to be patient and let your cat become used to handling and having their mouth touched; don't introduce a toothbrush until your cat is ready for the next stage. If they show signs of aggression, stop immediately.

When your cat is comfortable, put a small amount of toothpaste on a toothbrush designed for cats - these have angled handles and softer bristles. When brushing, the back teeth are usually the most difficult to reach but the most important to clean.

To make the experience enjoyable, reward your cat with a dental treat or their favorite toy to play with afterwards.

16

# Cat Grooming Needs

Cats are excellent groomers. They have built-in tools including their tongue, which is covered with hundreds of tiny hooks called papillae; these allow cats to get saliva right down to their skin and keep themselves clean.

But despite being excellent groomers, cats still need extra grooming from their owners to maintain a healthy, shiny coat and to prevent hairballs and fur matting. How often a cat needs to be groomed will vary between each individual cat, but frequency should generally increase during shedding seasons and with medium- and long-haired cats. It's recommended to groom long-haired cats daily, while short-haired cats may only require grooming about once a week.

Brushing your cat improves the overall condition of their skin by removing dirt, grease, and dead hair, while stimulating blood circulation. It also provides you with an opportunity to check for fleas, skin problems, injuries, lumps, and bumps. Cats generally don't need to be bathed, unless they become very dirty or need a veterinary-prescribed medicated bath for a skin disease.

Ideally, you should start grooming your cat at a young age to get them accustomed to it.

Avoid forcing or restraining your cat as this can cause a negative association with grooming, making future attempts more stressful. If your cat resents being groomed and you feel it is unsafe to do it at home, it's best to make an appointment with a professional groomer or a veterinarian to avoid potential injury to you or your cat.

17

# How to Safely Trim Your Cat's Nails

Trimming your cat's nails every few weeks is an important part of maintaining their health and protecting your furniture. Most cats don't like having their paws touched or claws trimmed, so starting nail trims at a young age, and offering treats to make it a positive experience, can get them used to the process.

Try resting your cat in your arm or on your lap or place them on a table and lift one paw at a time. If you have a helper, they can hold or distract the cat with treats and pats while you clip. Cats have retractile claws, so you'll need to gently press your cat's toe pad to extend the claw.

Most cats have light colored claws, making it easy to see the pink area that contains nerves and blood vessels, called the "quick". Using designated cat clippers, the claw should be cut approximately 2 mm away from the quick. The quick is very sensitive, so when in doubt, cut less. If the quick is cut, apply pressure to the very tip of the claw and dip the paw in styptic powder or cornstarch, or gently press the nail on a bar of soap.

Don't worry about trimming all claws at once; few cats remain patient for more than a few minutes, so you may need to complete the rest later. If you need help with trimming your cat's nails, visit your local veterinary clinic.

18

# Fleas, Worms & Other Parasites

Regular parasite prevention is an essential part of good pet ownership. Fortunately, there are many pet parasite preventatives available that will keep you and your pets safe. This means there are a lot of options to choose from, but this can also lead to confusion. Which option is best?

There are two categories of parasites to protect your pets against: endoparasites and ectoparasites. Endoparasites are organisms that live inside their hosts, while ectoparasites are organisms that inhabit the host's external surfaces.

Endoparasites that affect cats include heartworm, tapeworm, hookworm, and roundworm. (Heartworm is transmitted through mosquitoes, which are everywhere, making it important to have year round heartworm protection.) Ectoparasites of concern include fleas, ticks, and mites.

Regardless of whether your cat is kept indoors or outdoors, it's important they are treated year-round, because these parasites can easily find their way into your home via insects or by traveling on you or your other pets.

For any given parasite there are several preventative options. Many products treat more than one parasite, but none treats them all, so using a combination of products is common.

These products come in many forms, including a topical or spot-on treatment which involves applying a liquid to your cat's skin that will spread across their body, localizing in the fatty/oily layer of the skin and fur. Other options include tablets or infused collars.

It is not safe to treat your cat with dog flea treatment; dog treatments can contain a chemical called permethrin, which is toxic to cats.

For advice on which parasite preventative is best for your pet, please consult your veterinarian for more details.

# 19

# Wet vs Dry Food

When it comes to cat food, the options are plentiful. Cats should be fed according to their life stage or specific health conditions' needs; kittens require more protein and calories, senior cat foods have lower phosphorus levels to support aging kidneys, and cats with skin conditions can benefit from diets enhanced with fatty acids.

Both dry and wet cat food have pros and cons. Because wet foods typically contain more than 60 percent water (the moisture content of the prey that cats have evolved to eat) they may be a good option for cats that don't readily drink water. They can be beneficial for cats prone to urinary tract disease: wet foods dilute urine, lowering the concentration of inflammatory elements in the bladder. Wet foods' higher water content also means a lower energy density than dry food, which may be beneficial for cats that are overweight or frequently constipated.

It's cheaper to manufacture dry food, so for the same cost per meal, dry food is usually a better-quality option. Dry food may be a good option for cats that like to graze over the day, as it can be left out for longer periods. Dry foods tend to be easier to use in food dispensers, food toys, and puzzle feeders, and some dry diets can reduce tartar build-up. Cats fed dry food diets should always have fresh, clean water available to promote water intake.

## 20

# How to Tell if Your Cat is Overweight

Obesity in pets is an incredibly important issue - overweight animals are at increased risk for developing serious weight-related disorders such as diabetes, arthritis, high blood pressure, kidney disease, cancer, and more.

A cat at an ideal weight will have ribs that are not visible but easily felt. They will have an obvious waist, minimal amount of abdominal fat, and a slight abdominal tuck when viewed from the side. Once cats have fully grown, they should maintain a stable weight.

**TIP**

Replace high-calorie treats with cooked zucchini to aid weight loss while keeping your cat feeling full and satisfied.

A cat that is too thin will have pronounced, easy-to-feel ribs, spine, or pelvis. They will have a marked abdominal tuck and loss of body muscle. A cat that is starting to put on too much weight will have ribs that are not easy to feel, moderate fat covering, and a rounding of their belly. An obese cat will have a ribcage that is very difficult to feel, marked abdominal fat, fat within their groin, and no waist.

If you're concerned about your pet's weight, you can visit your veterinarian for a weight assessment. An annual veterinary weight check is important to detect any inappropriate weight changes, investigate underlying health concerns, and to seek advice on weight management. It's much easier to prevent excess weight gain than it is to lose excess weight.

# 21

# Creating a Weight Loss Plan

Before jumping into a new feeding schedule and diet, consult with your veterinarian to determine how much weight your cat needs to lose.

The goal of weight loss is for your cat to steadily lose between one to two percent of their body weight per week through developing healthy habits. If cats lose too much weight too quickly, this can result in nutritional deficiencies and health issues. Overweight cats that go even two days without eating can develop fatty liver disease, which can result in liver failure if left untreated. By partnering with your veterinarian, you can develop a plan to help your cat lose weight in a healthy way.

Because weight loss is based on the principle that energy expenditure needs to be greater than caloric intake, it may seem like a good idea to simply reduce the amount of food your cat is given daily. However, this is not recommended: it can encourage poor behavior like aggression or begging and may result in nutritional deficiencies. Veterinary prescription diets are specially formulated to help your cat lose weight; they generally contain high-quality protein for fat metabolism and energy, and a high fiber content to help your cat feel fuller with a reduced caloric intake.

When introducing a new diet to your cat, allow about a week to transition by adding a small amount of the new food and subtracting an equal amount of the old food each day; this will minimize digestive upsets.

## 22

# Tips to Help Your Cat Lose Weight

Weight loss requires multimodal lifestyle intervention; while diet is a major component of weight loss, increasing physical activity helps burn calories.

Play with your cat for 30 minutes a day using a variety of toys; this will strengthen your bond and help them stay active. Cats also enjoy fetch, and something as simple and cheap as scrunched-up paper can be used.

You can also encourage them to use puzzle feeders, treat toys, a feeding ball, or move their food around the house so that they must seek it out and do some extra walking.

Treat toys make your cat trade physical activity for food. They turn mealtime into playtime, providing both mental and physical stimulation. Food puzzles ensure your cat eats slower for better digestion and will feel fuller faster (adding water to your cat's food can help achieve this).

Feed your cat over two or three meals throughout the day, rather than one meal. Giving them more opportunities to eat will keep them from feeling hungry. You can use an automatic feeder, which releases food at preset times. This ensures consistent amounts and removes your association with meals, stopping whining.

If you have multiple cats, separating them into different rooms for meals or using a microchip feeder is an option.

## 23

# Vegan Diets are Not Safe for Cats

It's understandable that vegetarians or vegans may feel uncomfortable with feeding their cat animal products. However, it's important to be aware of the risks that vegan diets pose to your cat's health.

Cats are obligate carnivores, meaning they require meat in their diet to fulfill specific nutrient requirements. Taurine is an amino acid essential for our health and heart function. Humans can get taurine from the protein sources we eat, or we can produce our own; cats cannot make their own taurine and must obtain it through the ingestion of animal sources.

Meat also provides cats with several other essential dietary substances, including the amino acid arginine, the fatty acid arachidonic acid, and vitamins A, B, and D. While humans can make vitamin D, cats must get it from their diet, and it comes predominately from animal sources. If cats don't receive these essential nutrients, they can suffer from heart disease, vision problems, weakened bones, poor musculature, and other health issues. Even with synthetic supplementation, a balanced diet that fulfills all your cat's nutritional needs without meat is exorbitantly difficult to produce. So, if you choose to adopt a vegan lifestyle, your cat's health is at serious risk if you also change its diet.

24

# The Risks of Raw Meat Diets

Negative feelings about commercial pet foods, flashy marketing, and anecdotes from friends lead some pet owners to feed their cats raw food diets.

Many pet parents have heard that raw foods are a cure-all for concerns ranging from allergies to dental problems, arthritis, and even cancer. However, there is ample evidence of nutritional deficiencies from raw diets and contamination of raw food with bacteria and parasites.

Raw meats are often contaminated, even if intended for human consumption, which puts your pet at risk - it is assumed people will cook their meat, making reasonable levels of contamination for human food safe.

It is important to know that feeding raw food to your cat comes with risks. Raw simply means uncooked, and these diets encompass many types of foods including uncooked meat, internal organs, bones, eggs, and milk. These diets may be commercial or home-made and are usually based on opinion, not evidence. Most pet owners who feed their pets raw food get their suggestions and information from breeders, neighbors, and websites run by individuals who are neither veterinarians nor qualified to offer advice on animal nutrition.

The manufacturers of the leading premium cat foods invest many resources and hundreds of thousands of dollars into research and development. They have vast amounts of data, and the leading veterinary bodies around the world all endorse their findings.

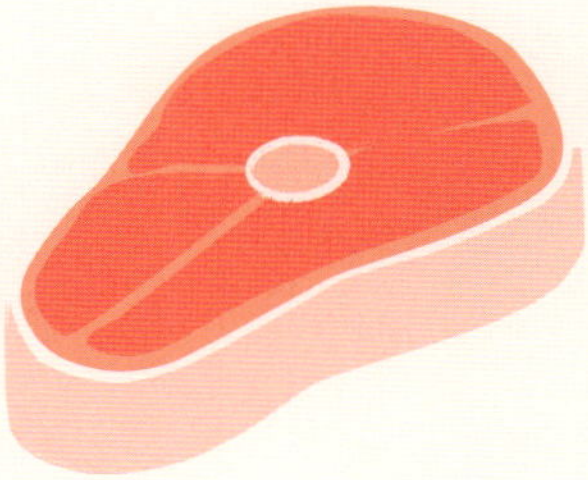

## 25

# Why Do Cats Love Boxes?

Owners are often bewildered when they buy their cat a fluffy new bed or a cool new toy, only for their cat to be more interested in the packaging.

Cats are solitary animals. Unlike dogs who tend to run in packs, cats tend to live alone and don't have anyone else to serve as a lookout. Although they may be a predator species, cats are still vulnerable to attacks or ambushes while they rest, so small, enclosed spaces that they can hide in make them feel safe and secure. Cats like boxes because they reduce stress and offer a safe zone where your cat can observe but not be seen.

Boxes are also great for warmth; cardboard is a good insulator, and the small space allows your cat to curl up and relax in a comfy, warm place. Cardboard also offers the perfect texture for your cat to bite, scratch, and play with.

Cats are famously curious creatures, so when a new item like a box comes into the house, expect that they will want to investigate it.

# 26

# Why Cats Purr

Cats purr for various reasons. They use these low frequency rumbles to communicate when they are happy, hungry, injured, or frightened, and as a form of self-soothing and healing. Understanding your cat's purrs can help you communicate better and strengthen your bond.

Cats begin purring when they are a few days old, primarily to let their mothers locate them for feeding time. This behavior continues into adulthood - cats purr to attract attention when they want food or to signal their contentment. By paying attention to your cat when they purr, you'll reinforce that behavior and they'll likely repeat it in the future, to solicit food or affection.

When cats are stressed or injured, the low-frequency vibrations of purring help them ease their breathing and soothe tension. The frequency at which domestic cats purr can improve bone density, promote tissue regeneration, and may even reduce pain.

So how can you tell why your cat is purring? Look at their body language and the context; if they are lying on your lap, eyes closed, tail relaxed, leaning into pats, they're likely signaling that they're happy. If they're purring first thing in the morning, they may be asking to be fed.

**TIP**

Cats purr to express contentment, soothe stress, and even heal themselves through low-frequency vibrations.

# 27

# Why Do Cats Scratch?

For cats, scratching is a normal, instinctual behavior and need. Cats scratch to express emotions like excitement or stress and to mark objects with the scent glands in their paws. Scratching provides your cat with an opportunity to stretch, exercise, and maintain their claw growth.

This is why cats often scratch furniture; it's a way of marking their territory and letting others know they live there. This is completely natural behavior, so it's important not to punish cats for scratching. Instead, provide them with the resources to scratch safely and happily, without damaging your furniture.

Provide your cat with something to scratch that, from their point of view, is more desirable than your furniture. The perfect scratching post will be sturdy enough that the cat can lean their whole weight against it, and tall enough that they can stretch up to their full height. Scratching boards can also be a great option, as many cats like to lie down while they scratch.

Place the scratching post in a location where the cat wants to scratch – if your cat enjoys scratching the couch, place the post beside it. When introducing your cat to a new post, play around it with a toy or rub catnip on it to encourage your cat to interact with it.

## 28

# How Often Should Your Cat Visit a Vet?

Your pet needs regular check-ups to stay healthy. The frequency of these visits depends on their age, health, and whether they are due for a vaccination. Cats tend to need more medical attention in the first year of their life and again as they enter their senior years.

In the first year, your kitten will likely visit a vet at least four times for a series of three vaccinations and to be spayed or neutered. At these visits, your vet will examine your kitten to make sure they're growing well and for any signs of illness.

After your kitten has stopped growing and matured socially, they are considered an adult. During this stage of your cat's life, you may only need to visit the vet once a year, depending on their overall health.

Your vet will thoroughly examine your cat from head to tail, recommend dental procedures or administer vaccines if required, and perform bloodwork or other tests to investigate any potential problems. Annual health checks are vital for your cat's health because they allow vets to diagnose, treat, and even prevent problems before they become life-threatening.

For senior cats, around 11 years of age and onwards, twice-yearly check-ups are recommended. In addition to routine vaccinations and health exams, senior pets may require blood and urine tests as they are likely to develop diseases such as kidney disease, thyroid problems, diabetes, arthritis, and cancer.

# 29

# Reducing Stress at the Vet Clinic

**Here are a few tips to help reduce anxiety around vet visits.**

**Carrier training:** By using treats, your cat can be trained to enter their carrier voluntarily. You can also take practice car rides; briefly drive around the block and reward them with praise and a treat after to get them accustomed to travel.

**Positive reinforcement:** Starting when they're young, you can train your cat to accept touch by gently handling their head, feet, and face, using food as a reward. When the veterinary staff need to examine your cat later, your cat won't be so nervous. You can also bring high reward treats to make the experience more enjoyable for your pet.

**Be positive:** Cats can sense when we are anxious or frustrated, which may influence their mood. By acting calmly and speaking in a soft voice before, during, and after the visit, your cat will feel more relaxed.

**Nutraceuticals and pheromones:** To calm your pet, cat-appeasing pheromone sprays can be sprayed on their carrier and blanket 30 minutes before departure. Over-the-counter nutraceuticals can also be used prior to stressful events.

**Call ahead:** Notify the vet staff of your concerns ahead of time – they may schedule an early appointment, or escort you directly to a quiet exam room, avoiding the waiting room. Cat-only clinics don't have the smells of other animals and are generally quieter and less stressful for cats.

## 30

# Cat Vaccines

Regular vaccination is an important part of routine feline health care and helps to ensure your beloved companion remains fit and well.

Vaccines work by exposing the body's immune system to a particular part of an infectious agent. This stimulates their immune system to recognize the infectious agent, so that when it is encountered again, the body will mount a very rapid and strong immune response to prevent the animal from getting sick.

Core vaccines protect animals from severe, life-threatening diseases that have global distribution and that all cats, regardless of circumstances or geographical location, should receive. For cats, these core vaccines protect against feline panleukopenia (parvovirus) and cat flu (feline calicivirus) and feline herpesvirus. This combination is commonly known as the F3 vaccination. If rabies is endemic to your region, it is also considered as a core vaccine.

The use of non-core vaccines is determined by geographical location, lifestyle, and exposure risk; these may include those that protect against feline leukemia virus (FeLV), feline immunodeficiency virus (FIV), Chlamydia felis, and Bordetella bronchiseptica.

The most common vaccine reactions are mild and may include sleepiness, decreased appetite, a slight fever, and swelling at the vaccination site. These signs should resolve within a few days; any adverse effects should be discussed with your vet. However, the benefits of protection against diseases outweigh the risks of potential side effects.

**TIP**

Bring your cat's favorite treats or food to the vet to create a positive, more enjoyable experience during their vaccines.

## 31

# Why Do Kittens Need So Many Vaccines?

Most kittens will be given their first vaccination around the age of six to eight weeks, before you bring them home, but it is vital to ensure their vaccination certificate confirms this.

Kittens need a total of three vaccinations given four weeks apart due to maternal antibody interference; kittens have temporary protection against many diseases, thanks to the antibodies they receive from their mother's milk within the first few days after birth. However, these maternal antibodies decline within a few weeks, after which kittens need vaccinations to build their own immunity.

While the maternal antibodies are circulating in the kitten's system, they can interfere with the way the vaccine works, but the exact age that an individual kitten will lose its short-term immunity is difficult to determine. So, kittens are vaccinated several times to ensure maternal antibodies can no longer interfere with proper immunization, without leaving the kitten susceptible to disease.

The immunity from kitten vaccinations weakens over time: your pet will need a booster vaccine. At your cat's annual health check, your veterinarian can advise you on which immunizations are required for your pet.

# 32

# Desexing Cats Saves Lives

A mature entire female cat can produce up to three litters a year, averaging 12 kittens per year. Among the surviving kittens, about half will be females, who are also capable of getting pregnant after their first heat, which can occur as young as four months of age.

Over her reproductive life, one female cat can have more than 100 kittens. If each female from every litter has that many kittens, a single pair mating can result in an astounding total of hundreds of thousands of kittens in less than ten years.

Desexing your cat prior to puberty prevents unwanted litters that contribute to the homeless cat population and burden on animal shelters. Most cats surrendered to shelters are under six months of age, often because of unwanted litters. Neutering cats, called castration in males and spaying in females, helps reduce this overpopulation, in addition to reducing the risk of certain diseases.

Desexing doesn't just save cats, though; it is an important measure to save vulnerable wildlife. The unowned cat population poses a serious threat to native wildlife populations due to cats' natural hunting instincts.

# 33

# Castrating Male Cats

As part of the battle against pet overpopulation, it's recommended for male cats not intended for breeding to be neutered.

Neutering males, also known as castration, reduces unwanted litters and unnecessary euthanasia. Performed under general anesthetic for safety and pet comfort, it involves removing both testes through a small incision into the scrotum. Usually, the incisions for cat castrations are so small that sutures are not required. Cats should be given a thorough physical exam to ensure they are in good health before the surgery.

Removal of the testicles will render your cat unable to reproduce and will result in decreased testosterone, and consequentially, in a reduction of unwanted behaviors and health issues.

A neutered male cat will be less likely to roam to find a mate, urine spray your home to mark their territory, and engage in fights with other males. Uncastrated male cats' potential for aggressive behavior puts them at increased risk of contracting serious infectious diseases such as feline immunodeficiency virus (FIV) and feline leukemia virus (FeLV), which are transmitted through cat bites.

They are also likely to suffer from fight injuries including cat bite abscesses, which are painful swellings of pus caused by bacteria.

Neutering should take place around four months of age, although it is generally safe for kittens as young as eight weeks of age to be neutered.

# 34

# Spaying Female Cats

An ovariohysterectomy, commonly called spaying, is recommended for female cats not intended for breeding. The procedure helps fight pet overpopulation and has health and behavioral benefits.

The surgical removal of a female cat's reproductive organs, which is performed under general anesthetic for their safety and comfort, involves the removal of the uterus and both ovaries. Cats should be given a thorough physical exam to ensure they are in good health before the surgery.

Cats have their first reproductive cycle (heat) around six months of age but can enter their first heat as young as four months of age. Females who have not been spayed will call to males about

every three weeks after coming into heat during sexually active times of the year until they become pregnant. An entire female cat will attract males to the area, resulting in urine spraying and fighting among males. Entire cats are also more likely to wander from home to find a mate and may not return.

Spaying your female cat reduces these behaviors, along with the risk of mammary cancer and uterine infections.

It's a common misconception that female cats should have one litter before being spayed. Unless you intend to breed your cat, there is no need to wait until after your pet has a litter. Waiting exposes them to the risks of pregnancy and birthing difficulties and increases their risk of mammary cancer.

# 35

# Breeding Cats

Are you thinking about breeding your cat? There are important things to consider before making that decision.

Breeding cats is a time-consuming and occasionally heartbreaking endeavor. Responsible breeders need to devote their time to learning as much as possible about the breed, feline health, and what to expect. There is an overpopulation of cats, with many surrendered to shelters; responsible breeders should only breed cats out of a passion to improve the breed's standards, not just to increase its numbers or make a profit.

If you do decide to breed your cat, it's important to be objective. Every cat owner thinks that their cat is the best in the world, but you should evaluate your cat's overall health. This requires regular veterinary care, good nutrition, and screening for genetic problems including: polycystic kidney disease in Persian cats, spinal muscular atrophy in Maine Coons, and deafness in white cats.

Some breeds have been deliberately selected and bred for extreme physical characteristics. Cats with these heritable traits will have offspring with compromised health and welfare and should not be bred. These traits include severe brachycephalic features, folded ears associated with osteochondrodysplasia (Scottish Fold disease), and shortening of long bones (Munchkin cats).

Learn from experienced breeders and establish a relationship with a veterinarian to learn what to expect during pregnancy, labor, after birth, and how to recognize and respond to an emergency.

## 36

# Allergies in Cats

The most common allergies affecting cats can be divided into four main categories: fleas, food, inhalant, and contact.

Flea allergies are the most common. When cats with this allergy are bitten, an allergic response to the proteins in the flea's saliva occurs. These cats experience an intense itching sensation and may scratch or chew themselves, causing scabs and open wounds on their skin. A similar reaction may be seen with mosquito bites.

Food allergies in cats are caused by a reaction to certain foods – most commonly the protein component, such as beef or chicken. These reactions often present as itchy skin, vomiting, or diarrhea. Your veterinarian can help you determine which foods are causing this irritation and recommend an appropriate diet.

Inhalant allergies result from exposure to an environmental allergen such as pollen, grass, mold, smoke, perfume, or dust. Most cats that have an inhalant allergy are allergic to more than one allergen, making identification and elimination challenging. These allergies cause nose, eye, skin, and respiratory symptoms and may be seasonal or year-round. Treatment depends on the number and duration of your cat's allergies.

Contact allergies present as a skin reaction from contact with an irritating substance such as shampoo, flea treatment, or bedding. Removal of the irritating substance generally resolves the issue. However, identifying the allergen can be challenging.

If you suspect your cat has allergies, your veterinarian can help determine the cause and provide you with treatment options.

# 37

# Chin Acne

Feline acne is a common condition that primarily affects cats' chins. Their sebaceous glands produce an oily secretion, called sebum, to waterproof the hair and lubricate the skin. When cats rub their chin all over objects, these glands play an important role in scent marking; sebum is why you may see a brown stain on objects they often rub against.

If these glands become overactive, excessive greasiness and keratin production can lead to blocked hair follicles and the production of comedones or "blackheads". Secondary bacterial infections can lead to inflammation of the hair follicles and formation of pustules or "whiteheads".

Other causes of chin acne include stress, viral infection, immunosuppression, allergies, and poor grooming habits.

The most common sign of chin acne is black flecks on the chin, giving it a dirty appearance. Diagnosis is generally based on medical history and clinical signs, and treatment often involves improving hygiene.

The irregular surfaces or scratches in plastic bowls make them more prone to bacterial contamination - replacing plastic water and food bowls with metal or ceramic bowls may help. Your veterinarian may recommend cleaning the chin with antibacterial washes or medicated shampoo, applying a medicated ointment, or dietary supplementation with fatty acids to promote skin health. Stubborn cases may require additional diagnostic tests, therapies, or referral to a veterinary dermatologist.

**TIP**

Switch to stainless steel or ceramic bowls to prevent acne.

# 38

# Blocked Cats Are an Emergency

A "blocked" cat is a cat with a urinary blockage, which is a painful and life-threatening condition.

An obstruction in the urethra, the tube that drains urine from the bladder, causes a back-up of urine in the body. This can damage the lower urinary tract and cause kidney failure. This condition is more common in young to middle-aged male cats and may have several different causes including stress, obesity, lack of access to water, diet, infectious agents, and an indoor lifestyle.

Blocked cats usually strain repeatedly in the litter tray without passing urine, cry or howl, demonstrate increased agitation, lick their genitals, or hide because of discomfort. Eventually the pain becomes excruciating, and the bladder may even rupture from the build-up of pressure. As the urine flow stops, waste products begin to accumulate in the body and life-threatening electrolyte imbalances can occur.

It's important to recognize the signs early, as a delay in treatment can prove fatal. Blocked cats should be hospitalized immediately for emergency treatment.

Your veterinarian will make a diagnosis based on medical history, physical examination, blood and urine tests, and imaging such as x-rays or ultrasound.

Treatment involves inserting a urinary catheter to relieve the obstruction and empty the bladder, and correction of any biochemical abnormalities. Most blocked cats are hospitalized for several days.

# 39

# Inappropriate Urination

Your cat may be urinating outside their litter tray for several reasons, including medical and behavioral issues, or an aversion to their litter tray.

Medical causes include urinary tract infections or inflammation, bladder stones, or diseases that cause cats to drink and urinate more, such as diabetes or thyroid, kidney, or liver disease. Age-related disorders such as arthritis or cognitive decline may influence a cat's ability to use their litter tray. If any part of the urination process is painful or uncomfortable, it may cause cats to eliminate elsewhere.

A physical exam and urine analysis, as well as additional tests may be needed to determine if medical problems are a cause or contributing factor.

Cats may change their urination pattern out of frustration, stress, or anxiety. To determine the source, a detailed environmental and behavioral history will need to be obtained to evaluate litter tray size, number, and locations, the litter substrate used, litter maintenance, and potential stressors such as household changes.

Urine spraying, also known as marking, may also be the cause. Urine spraying allows your cat to surround themselves with their own familiar smell and marks their territory against a perceived threat.

Spraying can often be distinguished from other types of inappropriate urination because cats tend to lift their legs and spray on vertical surfaces. Undesexed males are more likely to mark, but neutered male and female cats can also spray if they feel threatened or stressed.

40

# Cat Bite Abscesses

Cats are territorial animals – they will fight to protect their territory from incursions by other cats. Neutering may reduce the likelihood that a cat will fight, as males are especially territorial. However, desexed cats may still get into fights, resulting in cat bites and abscesses.

Cats' mouths harbor bacteria, which can be injected under another cat's skin through biting. This can cause an infection in that area and a painful collection of pus called an abscess. However, the puncture wounds may not always be visible once the skin begins to heal, trapping the bacteria inside.

These abscesses most commonly occur on the face, neck, and tail. Clinical signs usually develop two to three days after a bite and may include swelling under the skin, limping, reduced appetite, or areas that are hot or appear painful when touched. If your cat develops an abscess, take them to the vet. They may lance and flush the abscess and may prescribe systemic antibiotics to rid the infection.

Cat bites can be dangerous to animals and humans. If you are bitten by a cat, you should immediately wash the wound under running water and see a physician as soon as possible.

## 41

# Feline Immunodeficiency Virus

Feline Immunodeficiency Virus (FIV) is a viral infection in cats that weakens their immune system, making them more vulnerable to other infections. Often compared to HIV in humans and referred to as "Feline AIDS", FIV is species-specific, meaning it only infects cats and cannot spread to humans. It spreads primarily through bite wounds, making outdoor cats or those in fights more at risk. It is not easily transmitted through casual contact, such as grooming or sharing food and water bowls.

Cats infected with FIV may not show symptoms for years. When signs appear, they can include chronic or recurrent infections (respiratory, skin, or urinary), weight loss, fever, poor coat condition, and diarrhea or digestive issues. Because symptoms are non-specific and vary between cats, regular veterinary check-ups and diagnostic testing are essential.

Keeping an FIV-positive cat indoors is crucial to prevent the spread of the virus and to protect them from infections. Regular veterinary check-ups, a balanced diet, and a stress-free environment are essential for managing their health. Raw food diets are not recommended due to the risk of bacterial contamination. Any signs of illness should prompt immediate veterinary attention and prevention is key.

Spayed or neutered cats are less likely to fight and spread the virus through biting, and keeping cats indoors minimizes their exposure to potentially infected outdoor cats. Testing new cats for FIV before introducing them to a household also helps protect other pets. Vaccination against FIV is available in some regions; discuss the risks and benefits with your veterinarian to determine if it's appropriate for your cat. Microchipping FIV-positive cats is vital to ensure they aren't mistakenly euthanized if lost or taken to a shelter.

While there is no cure for FIV, with the right care and precautions FIV-positive cats can live just as long and happily as non-infected cats. Education, regular veterinary care, and a loving home environment are key to managing this condition and ensuring a great quality of life for your feline companion.

## 42

# The Holiday Season & Your Cat

The holiday season is a festive time filled with family gatherings, music, and an abundance of food. However, it also presents risks to your cat.

Cats are sensitive to noise and may be shy around strangers, so it's best to provide them a quiet space where they can feel safe, but still have access to their bedding, fresh water, and their litter tray.

Toxins like onions, raisins, chocolate, and alcohol should be stored in facilities your cat cannot physically access.

Most cats, but especially kittens, enjoy playing with ribbons, string, and tinsel, but they can cause serious stomach and intestinal damage. So, it's best to keep tinsel off the tree and collect all ribbons and strings after gifts are opened.

Playful cats may try to play in Christmas trees or chew on electrical cords, especially if these cords contain sparkling lights. This puts them at risk of injury and electrocution. To avoid this, trees may need to be stored in separate rooms that can be blocked off from your cat, and lights hung out of reach of your pet with loose cords tightly secured.

Tree water can contain harmful fertilizers, and access to the tree's watering dish should be blocked off.

Ingestion of poinsettias and holly can cause intestinal upset. Some mistletoe species and all parts of lily plants can be extremely toxic to cats. These plants should be kept out of your home; you can choose non-toxic plants or use silk flowers instead.

## 43

# Grapes & Raisins Toxicity

Grapes and their dried varieties (raisins, sultanas, and currants) are healthy snacks for people, but they present a potential health threat to cats. Even a small number of grapes or raisins can cause your cat to develop kidney failure.

Initial clinical signs may present within 12 hours of ingestion; your cat may show symptoms of vomiting and hyperactivity. If these symptoms are left untreated, your cat can become lethargic, exhibit diarrhea, decreased appetite, and dehydration. More severe signs of kidney damage are not seen for days after ingestion – these symptoms include nausea, anorexia, vomiting, diarrhea, belly pain, bad breath, and excess thirst.

It's best to store grapes and raisins off countertops and other places accessible to your cat. Cat-proof locks may be necessary if there are curious kittens in the household. If your cat has consumed grapes, raisins, sultanas, or currants, take them to a veterinarian immediately. As with any toxin, the sooner the toxicity is diagnosed, the sooner decontamination and treatment can start, keeping your pet safer and the treatment's expenses down.

# 44

# Garlic & Onion Toxicity

Garlic and onions sizzling in a pan might have an appetizing aroma and delight our taste buds, but they can be toxic to cats. Onions, garlic, leeks, shallots, scallions, and chives are all part of the Allium plant family and can cause serious medical problems for your cat.

Although mild signs of clinical illness may occur soon after ingestion, the most severe consequences of toxicity are more likely to take several days to appear.

While the Allium plant family is typically poisonous to cats when consumed in large quantities, concentrated onion and garlic in soups or powders can also be toxic, resulting in anemia.

Anemia occurs when there is a lack of healthy red blood cells to carry oxygen to the body's tissues. It can result in pale gums, elevated heart rate, increased respiratory rate and effort, red-colored urine, weakness, and collapse.

The damage Allium toxicity does to red blood cells can also cause kidney damage, presenting as increased drinking, increased or decreased urination, vomiting, and decreased appetite.

Cats can be very clever and may gain access to food even when placed on higher surfaces such as countertops.

If your cat ingests any plant of the Allium family, you should take them to a veterinarian. Early decontamination and treatment reduce the risk of serious effects.

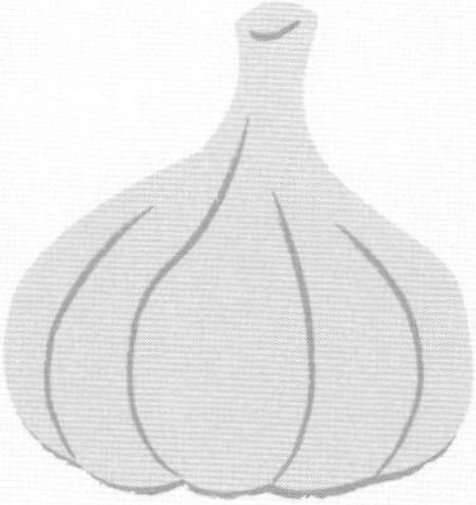

## 45

# Alcohol Toxicity

Products containing ethanol, isopropanol, or methanol can cause alcohol intoxication. We mostly think of alcohol as found in beverages. However, it is also in hand sanitizers, mouthwashes, liquid medications, fragrances, alcohol-flavored chocolates, auto fuel, and fermenting bread dough.

Exposure to alcohol, either orally or through the skin, can cause intoxication in cats. Clinical signs can occur as quickly as 15–30 minutes after exposure. The most common signs include vomiting, diarrhea, or weakness. In more severe cases, a low body temperature, low blood pressure or sugar, trouble breathing, slow reflexes, disorientation, tremors, coma, and death may occur.

It is important to contact your veterinarian as soon as possible after ingestion. Depending on the severity of symptoms, treatment will vary. Your veterinarian may induce vomiting if ingestion was recent, and your cat is not yet showing clinical signs. Intravenous fluids can help eliminate the alcohol and correct electrolyte abnormalities. In more severe cases, your veterinarian may need to offer assisted ventilation, seizure control, and other supportive therapies. In most cases of alcohol ingestion, if initial treatment is successful, symptoms should start to subside within 12 hours.

To keep your cat safe, be aware; cats may ingest alcohol because of unattended beverages or through exposure to cleaning products, mouthwash, or perfume containing alcohol. Alcoholic drinks made with milk are especially attractive to cats.

## 46

# Lily Toxicity

Cats are inquisitive by nature, and sometimes this curiosity can get the best of them. Cats may be drawn to a bouquet of colorful flowers, but if that bouquet contains lilies, this interaction may be lethal. Lilies are so toxic that a cat can suffer kidney failure from just biting a leaf, licking pollen from their paw, or drinking water from a vase containing lilies.

Ingesting any part of the plant can cause complete kidney failure in less than three days. Early signs of lily toxicity in cats may occur within 12 hours of ingestion and include lethargy, vomiting, drooling, and loss of appetite. Increased urination and dehydration are signs of kidney damage that may appear 12–24 hours after ingestion. Kidney failure can occur as early as 24 hours after ingestion and lead to death if left untreated. Delay can greatly impact treatment's success.

Owners should make sure their cats never have access to lilies of any kind. Around Mother's Day and Easter, these flowers are often included in bouquet gifts, which can lead to an increase in lily toxicity cases. Because these flowers are so dangerous for cats, it's best these plants are not brought into your home.

# 47

# Arthritis: Symptoms & Diagnosis

Osteoarthritis is a common disease in cats. As it is more common and severe in older cats, any cat over seven years of age should be examined by a veterinarian for signs of pain, discomfort, or other changes affecting certain joints.

Arthritis is a chronic degenerative disease caused by deterioration of the cartilage protecting the joint's bones; this results in inflammation and friction between the bones, causing pain and decreased mobility. The most affected joints are the shoulders, hips, knees, elbows, lower back, and ankles.

Signs of arthritis include muscle loss and reduced mobility, which can present as reluctance to jump up on or down from surfaces or climb stairs. Cats may exhibit reduced activity; they may spend less time playing and interacting with members of the household and more time sleeping. Cats suffering from arthritis may spend less time grooming themselves and have a matted coat as a result. Alternatively, cats may over-groom painful joints, leading to hair loss in those areas. Arthritic cats may exhibit behavioral changes and become more irritable when handled or patted, have less patience with other animals, or spend more time alone.

If you suspect your cat may be exhibiting signs of arthritis, it's important to consult with your veterinarian. Arthritis is generally diagnosed through a review of the changes observed at home and during a physical examination.

# 48

# Arthritis: Management & Medical Treatment

Arthritis treatment is multimodal, meaning several therapies are used in combination to attain the best outcome.

Modifying the home environment can greatly improve a cat's quality of life. Providing soft plush bedding in easy-to-access and warm areas of the home will help them stay comfortable. Cats enjoy elevated spaces, but those with arthritis will not be able to make big jumps; ramps or smaller steps will allow them to reach these areas more easily. Food, water, and litter trays should be in easy-to-access locations, and litter trays should have one low side for entry. Arthritic cats may also need additional grooming and nail trimming.

Osteoarthritis is a progressive disease. Prevention through weight management, dietary supplements, medical management, and additional therapies are the best ways to keep your cat's joints healthy.

Weight control prevents and manages the disease; a lean, healthy body avoids putting extra stress on the joints. Dietary supplements containing essential fatty acids may reduce inflammation.

Medical management typically focuses on slowing down the development of the disease, managing pain, decreasing inflammation, increasing mobility, and improving quality of life. The most common class of drugs used to manage arthritic pain are non-steroidal anti-inflammatory drugs (NSAIDs). Additional treatment may include injections to delay the progression of disease and acupuncture.

# 49

# Chronic Pain in Cats

Has your cat been acting differently? Have they been keeping to themselves more or acting irritable? For many of cats' behavioral problems, pain is an underlying or contributing cause.

Cats had a long history in the wild before becoming pets. To survive, they evolved a deep-seated instinct to hide pain; a cat in pain is seen as weak in the wild, putting them at risk of predation, so they hide their discomfort.

Chronic pain is the most common type that cats experience. In this category, dental and arthritis pain occur most commonly.

**TIP**

Cats are stoic and often hide their pain. Subtle changes like reduced jumping, changes in grooming, or litter box habits should be investigated by your vet.

Arthritis pain affects most cats over 12 years of age. It may present as changes to their physical activity and/or their behavior. Cats may sleep more, move away from pats, or cry, scratch, and bite during handling.

Many cats with dental pain will not show outward signs; cats with dental disease will not always stop eating, despite experiencing pain. A cat's mouth must be opened and examined to see if disease is present.

Cats are amazing, and it's up to us to keep them that way, especially in their older years. If you're ever worried about your cat, take them to a veterinarian.

# 50

# Saying Goodbye & Remembering Your Pet

Caring for a cat means preparing for all stages of life, from raising a kitten to attending to an aging or unwell senior.

Determining the right time to pursue euthanasia can be a tremendously difficult decision for pet owners, but your veterinarian can work with you to assess your pet's quality of life. If your cat's problems are treatable, early intervention can reduce suffering, and many signs of old age, like arthritis, can be relieved. When other means of alleviating pain and distress are no longer helpful and your pet's quality of life is affected, however, a veterinarian may recommend euthanasia, which is a humane way of inducing death.

Assessing your pet's quality of life is subjective and dependent on your cat's disease progression, their personality and comfort, and your personal beliefs. Pain and anxiety are two of the most important aspects of veterinary hospice care. Persistent and incurable diseases, inability to eat and/or maintain personal hygiene, difficulty breathing, and lack of interest in activities previously considered enjoyable may be indications that euthanasia should be considered.

Losing someone you love is devastating and it's important to allow yourself to grieve. We all respond to loss differently; you may want to consider engaging in self-care activities, or in mourning practices such as creating a memorial, photo album, or video collage, and talking to others who relate and can help you through the grieving process.

It's never easy to lose a pet, but it is possible to find peace after loss and reflect on the memories you shared that will forever live in your heart.

Smith Street Books

Published in 2025 by Smith Street Books
Naarm (Melbourne) | Australia
smithstreetbooks.com

Distributed outside of ANZ, North & Latin America by
Thames & Hudson Ltd., 6–24 Britannia Street, London, WC1X 9JD
thamesandhudson.com

EU Authorized Representative: Interart S.A.R.L.
19 rue Charles Auray, 93500 Pantin, Paris, France
productsafety@thameshudson.co.uk; www.interart.fr

ISBN: 978-1-9232-3912-8



Smith Street Books respectfully acknowledges the Wurundjeri People of the Kulin Nation, who are the Traditional Owners of the land on which we work, and we pay our respects to their Elders past and present.



Publisher: Paul McNally
Editor: Lucy Grant
Text: Dr. Marlena Lopez
Design, illustrations and layout: Hannah Naughton
Proofreader: Pamela Dunne

Text in this book previously appeared in *Coaching Cards for New Cat Parents*.

Printed & bound in China by C&C Offset Printing Co., Ltd.

Book 395
10 9 8 7 6 5 4 3 2 1

FSC www.fsc.org
MIX
Paper | Supporting responsible forestry
FSC® C008047